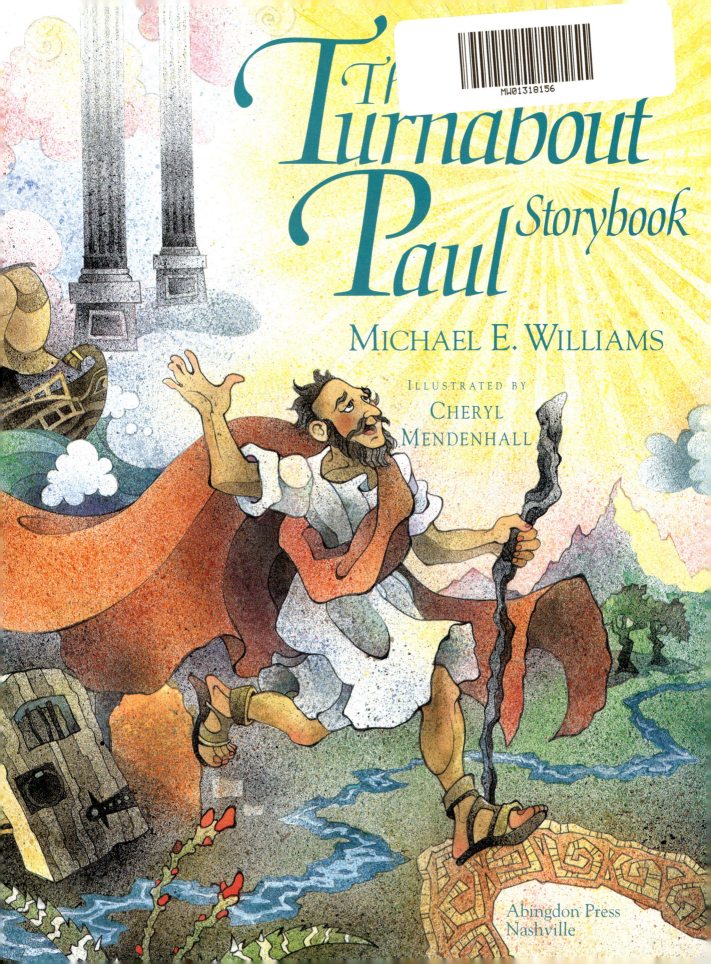

THE TURNABOUT PAUL STORYBOOK

Copyright © 1995 by Abingdon Press

No part of this work may be reproduced or transmitted in any form or by any means, electronic or mechanical, including photocopying and recording, or by any information storage or retrieval system, except as may be expressly permitted by the 1976 Copyright Act or in writing from the publisher. Requests for permission should be addressed to Abingdon Press, P. O. Box 801, 201 Eighth Avenue South, Nashville, TN 37202.

This book is printed on recycled, acid-free paper.

ISBN 0-687-00793-3

For Sarah and Elizabeth

95 96 97 98 99 00 01 02 03 — 10 9 8 7 6 5 4 3 2 1
MANUFACTURED IN HONG KONG

Contents

A Word from Saul's Teacher 4

The Example of a Good Man 7

Turnabout Paul 13

What You Must Do to Be a Christian and Other Arguments 16

Priscilla and Aquila 19

Lydia 21

God's Prison Break 25

Paul and the Philosophers 30

Staying Calm in the Storm 33

Paul at Rome 37

CHAPTER ONE

A Word from Saul's Teacher

In which our hero's teacher describes some personality quirks in our hero.

My name is Gamaliel, and I was Saul's teacher. Of course that was before he became known as Paul. He was a good student and always good for an argument. He would argue all day long and into the night, if he thought he was right. He came from a city in Asia Minor called Tarsus. He learned from his family at home, and he must have learned from the university in Tarsus.

He was also a Roman citizen. How his family came to receive such an honor, I do not know, but it was a great advantage, especially for someone of the Jewish faith. It meant Paul

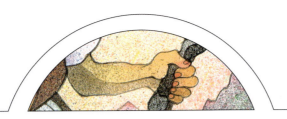

could not be beaten or jailed by just anyone. If he wanted, he could ask the emperor to decide any case the people in power might bring against him in court. He was a man of two worlds, you might say. He was Jewish through and through, and very loyal to his religious heritage. He was also a Roman by citizenship, which most of us Jewish folk were not. This meant he was given special treatment when the going got rough for us.

We knew he was special, and, believe me, he knew he was special. He was fond of mentioning his Roman citizenship in a casual way. Some of the students thought he meant to rub in his citizenship, something they didn't have. I don't think that was the case, though I might be wrong. But it was not just his citizenship that made him stand out in a crowd.

While he was not the brightest student I ever taught, he stuck the longest to his opinion in a dispute. The others would say, "He would argue with a signpost before there was a word on it." But they said that behind his back. He loved a good fight, not with fists, but with words. And he could win over smarter debaters by simply wearing them out. His opponents would give up before he would.

I remember when he decided that the followers of the rabbi named Jesus were a danger to our religion. He hunted them down without mercy and hounded them with arguments. He

would not personally harm anyone, but he had been known to stand back and hold the cloaks of those who would. But he knew that refusing to stop a violent act made him just as guilty as a murderer.

One day he came to me with his angry words and his ill temper telling me all the evil things these followers of Jesus were doing. He said that they threatened our whole way of life. I told him the same thing I had said to the ruling body of our people, among whom I am one.

"If this thing is from God," I said, "there is nothing we can do to stop it. If it is not from God, there is nothing they can do to make it work." I still stand by those words.

It wasn't long after that meeting that I heard our Saul had turned about in his opinion. Now people know him as Paul. He tells about being blinded on the way to Damascus, and only after he got his sight back could he see things clearly. That's Saul for you. Now he will argue for them with the same energy that he used against them before. I wonder what these followers of Jesus will make of his turnabout.

What will come of this, I do not know. Only God knows.

The Turnabout Paul Storybook

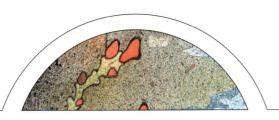

CHAPTER TWO

The Example of a Good Man

In which our hero overhears a sermon he would rather not have heard.

The crowd was angry because of a man named Stephen. He was a Jewish person who spoke Greek. He followed the teacher named Jesus. The crowd had been told that Stephen had said some terrible things about their ancestor Moses. So they brought Stephen before their leaders. The leaders asked him if what people were saying was true. Instead of answering with a simple yes or no, Stephen told a story.

"A long, long time ago in a land called Ur our God called Abraham and Sarah to leave their families and friends. They left their homes and everyone they knew to come to this land where we live now. After they were too old to have children

and had no child, God told them that their children and grandchildren and great-grandchildren would live in this land and that they would be a blessing to all people. But their lives would not be easy. For four hundred years they would be slaves in Egypt. Then one day they would return to this land and it would be their home.

"Sarah was ninety and Abraham was one hundred years old when their baby was born. They named him Isaac, which means *laughter*. They may have named him that because they were so happy he had finally arrived. Or because God chose such a strange and surprising time in their lives for him to be born. Either way, they could hardly believe it.

"Some time later Isaac's grandson Joseph was sold by his brothers into slavery and taken to Egypt. Joseph was his father's favorite son and never really had to work the way his brothers did. His brothers disliked him as much as their father loved him. Even after his brothers got rid of Joseph, God did not desert him. God helped Joseph in telling the king of Egypt what his dreams meant, and soon Joseph was second in power only to the king himself. Based on the king's dreams, Joseph came up with a plan to feed people throughout the world during a terrible famine. Among those he fed were his father and brothers. Joseph even brought his brothers to live in Egypt.

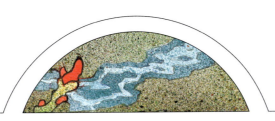

There they had plenty to eat, and they lived well. Joseph was certainly a blessing to all people, including his own family.

"Many years later, a king came to power who did not remember Joseph and all he had done for Egypt. This king made slaves out of Joseph's descendants, who were called Hebrews. Among these slaves, however, a baby named Moses was born. He lived with his family for three months. Then they put this little baby in a tiny boat made from reeds and put the boat in the Nile river. It happened that the king's daughter was taking a bath in the river. When she saw that the baby in the basket was alive, she took him and raised him as her own son. He grew into a wise and powerful man.

"When Moses was eighty years old, God spoke to him through a bush that burned but did not burn up. God told Moses to take off his shoes, since wherever God's voice was heard was a holy place. God broke the news to Moses that he was the one who would lead God's people out of slavery.

"Even though Moses was leading the people to freedom, the people had attitude problems. They said they had been better off as slaves in Egypt. Moses brought them safely through the Sea of Reeds, and they complained. They accused Moses of leading them out in the middle of nowhere to die.

"Then Moses went up on the mountain called Sinai to talk

The Example of a Good Man

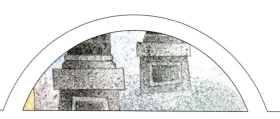

to God. After he had been gone a little while the people made a calf out of gold. Then they began to worship it instead of God, who had done so much for them. They still didn't understand."

And Stephen told the people more about the life of Moses. The story started getting long, and the religious people were getting a little tired of Stephen's story. This was their story, and they knew about Moses. At least, they thought they did. They wondered what Stephen was getting at. They didn't have to wait much longer.

Stephen continued, "You are just like the people who didn't understand what God was doing in Moses' time. They didn't want Moses to lead them, and now you don't want the one whom God has chosen. You might as well be dancing around a gold calf. Our ancestors stoned the prophets to death because they told the truth that people didn't want to hear. Our ancestors killed those who told us about the one God would choose to lead us, and you acted just like them when that chosen one arrived. God gave you the greatest of gifts, and you threw it away."

This made the crowds of religious people really angry. They dragged Stephen outside the city walls. You see, they weren't allowed to kill someone within the holy city. Then they stoned Stephen to death.

Even though the stones were bruising his body and breaking his bones, Stephen fell to his knees and prayed to God, "Do not hold what these people are doing against them. Forgive them."

Standing nearby was a young man named Saul. He was a student of religious law who had studied with the great teacher Gamaliel. Saul held the coats of those who were stoning Stephen to death. Saul saw Stephen die and heard him cry out to God to forgive the ones who were stoning him. Even so, we are told, Saul approved of putting this good man, Stephen, to death.

The Example of a Good Man

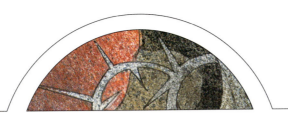

CHAPTER THREE

Turnabout Paul

*I*n which our hero goes blind,
trips, falls, hears a voice, and is called Brother.

Saul was angry, angrier than he had ever been. He was thinking mean thoughts as he walked toward Damascus. He thought, *The followers of Jesus were teaching that Jesus was the chosen one of God. Such rumors could not continue. After all, the chosen one of God would bring back a reign that had not been seen since the time of King David. No such thing had happened. Their teacher had died like a common criminal, nailed to a cross. Everyone had seen him die. Except his own followers, that is. Only the women had stayed to watch his death.*

The ones closest to Jesus were hiding. They deserted him in his time of trial. Except for the one who had turned him in. His followers were probably afraid the same thing would happen to them. And they would be killed, if Saul had anything to do with it.

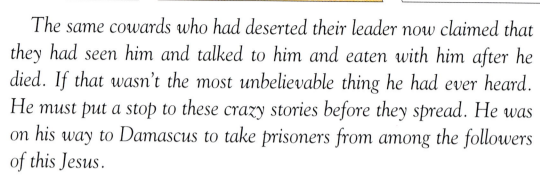

The same cowards who had deserted their leader now claimed that they had seen him and talked to him and eaten with him after he died. If that wasn't the most unbelievable thing he had ever heard. He must put a stop to these crazy stories before they spread. He was on his way to Damascus to take prisoners from among the followers of this Jesus.

Saul was in a world of his own thoughts when suddenly he felt a sharp pain in his eyes, as if he had suddenly looked directly into the blazing desert sun. But he had not looked in the direction of the sun. Now he could not see and could not tell where he was walking. He tripped and fell. He still could not see. What was the matter? Why would he suddenly go blind? What was the reason?

Then he heard the voice. At first he thought it was one of his companions coming to help him. The voice was gentle and sounded concerned. It said, "Why are you doing all these terrible things to me?"

That question threw his mind off balance just as the blindness had thrown his body to the ground. "Who are you?" Saul asked, expecting to hear a name he recognized. Instead that same gentle voice said, "I am Jesus, the one to whom you are doing terrible, terrible things. Get up and go to the city you were headed toward. Wait there, and I will tell you what to do next."

The other people who were traveling with Saul picked him up and led him into the city. After he arrived, blind and not sure of what to do, he waited for three days without eating a bite. After that long wait, in walked a man named Ananias. He was one of the followers of Jesus whom Saul had come to harm.

Ananias's voice trembled as he said, "Brother Saul."

Brother! He had called Saul *brother.* Wasn't he afraid of this man who had seen Stephen stoned to death? How could he call him *brother?*

"Brother Saul," the voice was steadier now. "The same Jesus who appeared to you as you traveled here told me to come to you so you might be able to see again."

At that very moment something like fish scales fell from Saul's eyes, and he was able to see the man who had called him brother. Saul was baptized and afterward ate and rested. He began to gain back his strength.

Soon Saul stood up among those who believed in God in Damascus and told them that Jesus was the chosen one of God. They could hardly believe their ears, since this was the man whom they feared just a few days before. What a turnabout!

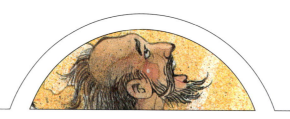

CHAPTER FOUR

What You Must Do to Be a Christian and Other Arguments

In which our hero disagrees with some friends.

Do you ever disagree with your friends? Paul disagreed with his friends often.

It may have started when he first wanted to join the followers of Jesus. After his turnabout on the way to Damascus, Paul began to tell that Jesus was the chosen one of God.

The people to whom he had been doing terrible things didn't trust him at first. You could understand that, couldn't you? When someone has done something cruel to you, it takes a long time to trust that the person might want to be nice

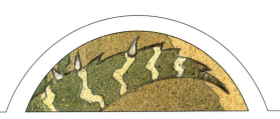

now. A man named Barnabas, whose name means *Son of Encouragement*, brought Paul to the followers of Jesus at Jerusalem.

Barnabas argued that Paul should be allowed to follow Jesus, too. Some were scared of Paul, and some just didn't want Paul around. Finally, they agreed with Barnabas, and Paul became a very important follower of Jesus.

Some time later the followers of Jesus argued about who should be allowed to follow Jesus and what should be required of them. Some thought that to follow Jesus you should become like Jesus and become Jewish. Paul had known many people who were not Jewish, called Gentiles. He had seen God at work in their lives, and Paul had baptized many of them. Paul believed that Jesus had opened the love of God to all people.

Peter, another follower of Jesus, had visited a Roman soldier named Cornelius. Peter had baptized Cornelius and the members of his family. They were all Gentiles. Baptizing Cornelius got Peter in trouble with the other followers of Jesus. Peter told them how God had brought him to the home of Cornelius, and many changed their minds. They began to suspect that God worked among the Gentiles, too.

Later Paul and Barnabas got into an argument over whether to take a young man named John Mark on a mission trip with

them. On an earlier trip John Mark had quit before Paul was ready to go home. We do not know why John Mark returned early. But Paul was angry with him and did not want to give John Mark another chance. Paul's attitude caused hurt feelings for Paul's friend Barnabas as well as for John Mark.

Barnabas may have remembered another young man known as Paul. He may have recalled that there were those who did not want to give Paul a second chance. After all, Paul had done more terrible things than John Mark ever dreamed of doing. Perhaps Paul had forgotten this earlier part of his life.

In any case Barnabas, the son of encouragement, took John Mark with him to Cyprus. Paul chose Silas, and they went to different parts of the world to teach people about Jesus.

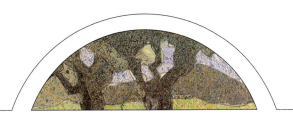

CHAPTER FIVE

Priscilla and Aquila

In which our hero makes a couple of new friends.

Jesus' followers had no church buildings during the time of Paul. Usually they met in houses. Worship in these homes included singing hymns, reading from the Hebrew Bible, telling stories about Jesus, and eating together. In Ephesus the followers of Jesus met in the home of Priscilla and Aquila, friends of Paul. Priscilla and Aquila probably led the services.

Priscilla and Aquila got to Ephesus in a roundabout, maybe even a turnabout way. As a Jewish couple, they were sent away from Rome along with all the other Jewish residents by an emperor named Claudius. They moved to Corinth, where they first met Paul. Later Priscilla and Aquila left Corinth and moved to Ephesus with Paul. Paul earned his living by making tents from cloth or working with the leather parts of tents. Priscilla and Aquila also made tents, which may be why Paul

decided to stay with them. They became good friends. They became such close friends that in one letter Paul says that this husband and wife had risked their lives to save his.

Priscilla and Aquila were partners in everything they did. They were partners in marriage. They were partners in business. They were partners in ministry. And Priscilla and Aquila were partners in ministry with Paul. Since Priscilla's name is mentioned first when the two are called by name, it is likely that she most often took the lead in their partnership. She may even have had a more important place in the society at the time.

They had plenty of money, and they were very generous with it. Priscilla and Aquila are seen by many as the kind of followers of Jesus that all people should be. They were loving, kind, and generous. They were willing to risk their lives for someone they loved. The way they worked together and loved each other was an example of God's love to Paul and to everyone who knew them.

Chapter Six

Lydia

In which our hero meets a stranger who becomes a friend, then a lifesaver.

Did you know that you could have girl friends who are not girlfriends, and boy friends who are not boyfriends? Girls and boys can be friends just as women and men can be friends. Paul mentions a number of women friends in his letters. Here is a story about a woman named Lydia who became a friend of Paul.

• • •

One day Lydia went to a place outside the city of Philippi where women gathered to say prayers. This place was near a river just outside the city. Lydia had not been born Jewish nor had she become Jewish. But she respected the God of the Jews, and she gathered with the women when they prayed at the

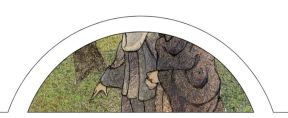

water's edge. On this day a man named Paul came to speak with the women there. Lydia came from a city named Thyatira, and she was a businesswoman. She sold purple cloth. She was probably wealthy. Purple was a color of distinction, royalty, and wealth. In those days only the most important people wore the color purple. Dyeing cloth the royal color was very expensive. In Thyatira, the people dyed cloth purple by using the root of a local plant named madder. In other Phoenician cities, people dyed cloth purple by using certain sea creatures.

Lydia already believed in the same God Paul worshiped, and when she heard him tell the stories of Jesus, she believed those too. She said she believed that Jesus was the one chosen by God to show God's love for all people. In this way she became a believer and follower of Jesus.

Then Lydia asked if she and everyone who lived in her house could be baptized. Paul agreed and baptized them. This wasn't unusual, since many people in families were baptized after only one family member chose to become a believer. Those baptized might have even included the servants who worked in her house.

Then Lydia asked if Paul and those with him would stay at her house while they were in Philippi. They agreed, and she

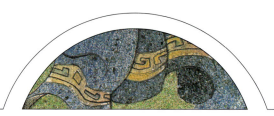

gave them a place to stay and food to eat. This meant that Paul would not have to earn money to live on while he was in Philippi and could spend all his time telling people about Jesus.

After Paul and Silas had been arrested, beaten, put in prison, and released from prison in a very surprising way, Lydia took them back into her home. Oh, but that is another story.

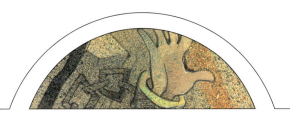

Chapter Seven

God's Prison Break

In which the jailhouse rocks.

The walls of the large prison were dark, damp, and cold. Paul's back burned and ached from the whippings he had been given. An ordinary person would have been terribly discouraged and sad.

Paul and his friend Silas had been thrown in prison for no good reason. Paul was a Roman citizen, and his captors should never have beaten Paul with a whip. It was against the law to whip a Roman citizen. Instead of moaning and crying, Paul and Silas were singing songs to God, praying and telling the other prisoners about Jesus.

Paul and Silas had been staying with their friend Lydia in Philippi. For several days in a row a slave girl had come up to them in the street and began to point and yell at them. She shouted, "These men are slaves of God. They speak of God's way."

What the slave girl said was true. Paul and Silas were there to speak for God. But the way the girl would shake all over, roll her eyes, and fling her arms about upset Paul. He said to her, "In the name of Jesus Christ I order you to come out of her."

Paul was not speaking to the girl at all. He was speaking to the spirit in her that made her so wild. At the very moment Paul spoke, the slave girl stopped shaking and shouting and became very quiet.

The slave girl returned to the house in which she served. The people who owned her became angry when they saw that she was not wild anymore. They made money through her. You see, the same spirit that made her wild also let her know the secrets of other people. After all she had seen that Paul and Silas served God without even knowing them.

Her owners made money when she foretold the future for other people. Now that the wild spirit was gone she could no longer make money for them by telling fortunes.

The slave owners went to the police and told them that Paul and Silas were troublemakers. "Paul and Silas are Jewish and foreigners and serve a foreign God," the owners told the police. So the police arrested Paul and Silas and beat them with a whip. The beating took place in public where anyone passing by could see. Then Paul and Silas were thrown into prison.

God's Prison Break

As Paul and Silas were singing, praying, and telling stories of Jesus, they felt the floor of the jail tremble. Then the walls began to move and the whole room shook. The other prisoners cried out because they knew they were going to die. But no one died that day. The earthquake was over and the cell was still standing. The prisoners looked around and saw that the door was open and the chains that were around their wrists and ankles had fallen away.

After the earthquake the jailer rushed to the prison. When he saw the cell door open and the prisoners free, he was about to kill himself. He would be in big trouble if the prisoners escaped. But Paul stopped the jailer from hurting himself. When he saw how Paul cared for him, the jailer asked, "What can I do to have the great love that you have, even for those who keep you in prison?"

Paul told the jailer, "Follow after the way of Jesus, and you will know that great love." So the jailer made a turnabout. He took Paul and Silas to his home. He washed their backs and put medicine on their wounds. Paul and Silas baptized the jailer and his whole family. Then they all ate together and were filled with peace and joy.

The next day those who had jailed Paul and Silas said they could go free. Paul argued that he was a Roman citizen and

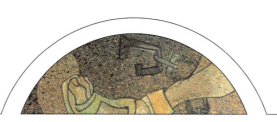

should never have been beaten or jailed. He said that he expected his release from prison to be done in front of the citizens of Philippi. After all, he and Silas had been beaten in public and thrown in prison so everyone could see. When those who put the two in prison heard that Paul was a citizen of Rome, they were afraid that they were in big trouble. So they came to Paul and Silas and said that they were sorry and asked them to leave town.

Paul and Silas went back to Lydia's house to meet with the other followers of Jesus. Then they went on their way.

CHAPTER EIGHT

Paul and the Philosophers

In which our hero thinks the thinkers need something to think about.

Paul had never seen so many statues of gods and goddesses. His religion called these statues idols or false gods. He knew he was not to worship them. Paul was walking in Athens, a city in Greece known for its learning. He was going to talk to people who worshiped these statues. He did not know if they really believed that the carved pieces of stone and the gold and silver figures were gods. Were they just pretending or were they serious? Paul had no idea.

Paul could read and write Greek so he read the words carved on the statues. Some statues had names; Asklepios—god of healing, Artemis—goddess of hunting, Demeter—god-

dess of growing things. The place where he would talk was called the Areopagus. It was named after Ares, the god of war. And many other statues stood tall in Athens.

Paul felt sad that so many smart people put their faith in statues made by human hands. They did not know that God made them and everything else that is. Paul was going to meet with the philosophers of the city. Philosophers are people who like to think. They also like to talk about what they have been thinking. Usually they like to talk to other philosophers. Paul didn't know what to expect, but he was ready to give the philosophers something to think about.

The philosophers who waited for Paul to arrive didn't know what to think of him either. Some said that he just babbled and didn't make any sense. Others added that he talked about gods that they had never heard of, gods from some foreign land. All the time Paul was telling the story of Jesus and the God of all people.

Paul said, "People of Athens, I can tell you are very religious. As I walked through your city I saw all the statues you worship. Along the way I saw on one altar the words, 'To the unknown god.' Let me to tell you about this God.

"The God who spoke the universe into being does not live in a statue of stone. The God who made you and me and

Paul and the Philosophers

everything that is cannot be made of silver or gold. The God who provides us with food and even breathed breath into our lungs doesn't need the food or incense you leave at your places of worship. God created the one ancestor from whom we all descended. God scattered us across the earth and made all the different peoples and nations. This God is very near us, and we are God's children.

"Because we are all God's children, we don't need to pretend that God lives in a statue of silver or gold or stone or anything else you can imagine. In the past God has overlooked our foolish worship. Most of us didn't know any better. Now God tells us to turn our lives around and look in a new direction. You see, God has chosen a just but merciful judge, and court is about to be called into session. Then the chosen one will judge how each of us measured up—or didn't. I'm here to tell you that God even raised this judge from the dead. His name is Jesus."

Most of the philosophers laughed and joked about what Paul said. A few philosophers asked to hear more about God and the merciful judge. Some of those became followers of Jesus. The Bible tells us that two of them were a woman named Damaris and a man named Dionysius.

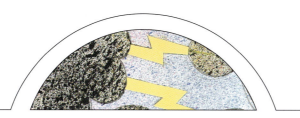

CHAPTER NINE

Staying Calm in the Storm

In which our hero doesn't flounder at sea.

The ship stopped rocking as easily as a baby's cradle and started tossing around like a leaf in a whirlwind. Paul knew they were in trouble. Big trouble! The wind stopped whispering and started to howl. The rain that had fallen gently now bounced off the ship. It seemed as if the sea had gone mad. All on board the ship with Paul were terrified.

Paul was a prisoner on the ship. He was on his way to appeal his case before Caesar. At first the sea voyage was easy. They sailed along the coast of Crete looking for a place to spend the winter before heading on to Rome. The winds were gentle, and the sea was smooth. Paul had warned the ship's owner and the captain that sailing during this time of year

could be dangerous. But they wanted to get to a better harbor, so they took a chance.

Now the sailors all thought, this is what comes of taking chances. The ship will break up, and we'll all drown. Then it won't matter who is the prisoner and who is the jailer. Then it won't matter who is the captain and who owns the ship. We'll all be under the water. They took the products that they had intended to sell in Rome and threw them overboard. They thought that would help. It didn't. Then they threw everything else off the ship. Only people and some food were left.

The storm continued for fourteen days. No one saw the sun during the day nor the moon and stars at night. They had all given up hope.

Paul told them, "You will all live through this. The ship will be lost, but no lives will go down with it. A messenger from God told me this and also told me that I will go before Caesar. We will get to land."

After two weeks, the sailors hoped that land would be near. They measured the depth of the ocean and found about 120 feet of water beneath the ship. They measured a second time and found only 90 feet of water. They knew they were coming close to land. They threw four anchors into the water and hoped that daylight would come soon. Some sailors wanted to

take a smaller boat to shore, but Paul warned them that they must stay aboard the ship if they wanted to survive.

As dawn broke across the sky, Paul convinced everyone to eat something since they would need the strength that food would give them. Paul took some hard bread, gave thanks to God, broke the bread and shared it with all 276 people onboard the ship. They all ate and felt better.

They saw a bay and knew that land was near, though they couldn't quite see land. They tried to make it to shore, but the ship stuck on a sand bar and began to break up. Some guards wanted to kill all the prisoners, but their leader wanted Paul alive so no one was killed. Paul told everyone who could swim to try to swim to shore. Paul suggested that those who couldn't swim hold on to planks from the ship. The planks would float and help them get to shore. Everyone did what Paul said and survived. They all arrived safely on an island called Malta.

CHAPTER TEN

Paul at Rome

In which our hero lives long, writes letters, and prospers.

Paul went to see the Jewish leaders in Rome after he arrived in the city. He told them that he had been jailed for no good reason. As a Roman citizen, he had asked Caesar, the ruler of Rome, to hear his case. The leaders told Paul that they had nothing against him. They had received no letter accusing him of doing wrong. They wanted to hear what he had to say.

So Paul told them stories about Jesus. Paul said that he believed that Jesus was the chosen one of God, the one who would actually be in flesh and blood God's love for all people. Paul believed that God's love included the Gentiles as well as the Jews. After they had listened to Paul, some agreed with him and some disagreed. No one tried to harm him or throw him in prison.

Paul lived in Rome for two more years and earned a living there. Anyone who came to his door was made to feel wel-

come, like an honored guest. He told people stories about Jesus. He told people about his own life and what God had done for him. No one tried to stop him from telling the stories of God's love.

Throughout his life Paul wrote letters to the followers of Jesus in other places. He never imagined that people would read these letters thousands of years later and would still learn about God's love from them. He simply told what he had learned from trying to follow Jesus and the God of love. What a turnabout for a man named Paul!

Paul at Rome